Special Days

Christmas

Rosemary Moore

WAYLAND

Special Days

Bonfire Night
Christmas
Easter
May Day
Mother's Day
Poppy Day

Editor: Elizabeth Gogerly
Series design: Kate Buxton
Book designer: Joyce Chester
Illustrator: Chris Molan
Photo stylist (cover): Gina Brown
Consultants: Jacqui Harrison and Rhona Perry of Stepping Stones

First published in 1999 by Wayland Publishers Limited,
61 Western Road, Hove, East Sussex, BN3 1JD

Find Wayland on the internet at http://www.wayland.co.uk

British Library Cataloguing in Publication Data
Moore, Rosemary
Christmas. - (Special Days)
1. Christmas - Juvenile literature
I. Title
394.2'663

ISBN 0 7502 2494 0

Typeset in England by Joyce Chester
Printed and bound by G. Canale & C.S.p.A in Turin, Italy

Picture Acknowledgements
The publishers would like to thank the following for allowing us to reproduce their pictures:
Bridgeman Art Library, London/ Pushkin Museum, Moscow 9/Private Collection 12/Bonhams, London 15; Chapel Studios/Zul *cover* (main); Mary Evans 11, 20; Eye Ubiquitous/David Batterbury 22/James Davis Travel Photography 8, 20, 23/Skjold *cover* (background); Ronald Grant Archive 21; Sally Greenhill 5, 27; Hulton Getty 26; Popperfoto 20, 30; Tony Stone 4, 27; Topham *title page*, 18, 19, 29; Wayland/Norfolk Museum Service 14.
The publisher would also like to thank the pupils and staff of St Mary Magdalen's School in Brighton
who acted as models for the front cover.

Contents

Celebrating Christmas

Many people around the world celebrate on the 25th December. This is Christmas Day, when people give each other brightly wrapped presents and eat special foods at tables decorated with candles and crackers.

▼ At Christmas all the members of the family come together to celebrate and exchange presents.

Why do many of us celebrate this day?

We remember it as the birthday of a baby called Jesus. He grew up to be a teacher and the founder of a great religion called Christianity.

▲ These schoolchildren are performing a special play to celebrate the birth of Jesus.

The Christmas story

Two thousand years ago, in the village of Nazareth, in the country now called Israel, an angel came to a young woman named Mary. She felt frightened, but the angel said, 'Do not be afraid. God has chosen you to be the mother of a very special child. He will be called Jesus and he will be known as the Son of God.'

6

Mary knelt before the angel and said she would do whatever God wished. When she looked up, the angel had gone.

Near the time of the baby's birth, Mary and her husband Joseph made a long journey to a town called Bethlehem.

The birth of Jesus

All the inns in Bethlehem were full but Mary and Joseph found a stable where they could sleep. That night, Jesus was born. Mary gently wrapped him up and laid him in a manger.

▼ This wood carving shows an angel guarding the baby Jesus and his parents.

Shepherds came to gaze in wonder at this special baby, born in a stable.

Shepherds in nearby fields saw a bright light. An angel appeared and told them about the baby Jesus. They hurried to the stable to see the baby.

Three wise men also visited Jesus. They wanted to see the child who was the Son of God. They took gifts of gold, frankincense and myrrh.

Winter festivals

In December in the northern half of the world the sun is low in the sky and days are cold. Long before the birth of Jesus, ancient people held winter festivals to persuade the sun to warm their crops and make them grow.

▼ People used to decorate their homes with ivy. They thought it was magic because it stayed green all through the winter.

During the Yule festival they decorated a huge log with ribbons and dragged it home to be burnt. They spread the ashes on their crops, believing this would make them grow better.

Nowadays, particularly in France, we sometimes eat a delicious chocolate cake called a Yule Log at Christmas time.

▲ These children are remembering the ancient custom of bringing in the Yule Log.

Christmas in Roman times

The Romans also held a festival in December. This was called Saturnalia. Later, when they became Christians, the Romans decided to celebrate Christmas at the same time as their festival of Saturnalia.

▼ The ancient Roman festival of Saturnalia was a time of celebration, with feasting, music and lots of dancing.

Early Christians decorated their homes with holly. This was because the prickles and berries symbolized the crown of thorns that Jesus wore when he died.

▼ Early Christians decorate their home at Christmas.

Christmas in the Middle Ages

In the Middle Ages Christmas was a huge celebration. Everybody had a two-week holiday. For poorer people this was usually the only holiday they had all year so they really enjoyed this special time.

▼ A king and his courtiers enjoy themselves at a special banquet to celebrate Christmas.

Three ladies of the Middle Ages singing a Christmas carol. Carols are songs about the birth of Jesus. Some of them have been sung for hundreds of years. ▶

Delicious foods were cooked. Meats that had been pickled and spiced earlier in the year were eaten in huge pies. These were followed by a tasty pudding made from dried fruit and porridge oats.

When Christmas stopped

There was a time when people stopped having fun at Christmas though. The Puritans, who ruled England, were Christians who believed that people should pray and work hard all year, even at Christmas. In 1644, the English Parliament banned festivals.

▼ The Puritans were very strict. Everyone had to work hard, even on Christmas Day, and celebrations were not allowed.

People were not allowed to sing carols. The Puritans banned all other kinds of merrymaking too. It was a long time before people enjoyed Christmas in the same way again.

A Victorian Christmas

The Victorians loved Christmas. For many it was a time for great celebrations. Rich people ate big meals with roast goose and plum pudding. The Victorians were also the first to pull Christmas crackers.

▼ This Victorian family are having great fun, playing a game of Blind Man's Buff.

▲ Victorians enjoyed sending each other Christmas cards.

▲ The royal family with their Christmas tree. Many Victorian families copied them by having fir trees in their homes too.

When Prince Albert came from Germany to marry Queen Victoria, he introduced the custom of bringing fir trees into the home and decorating them at Christmas.

19

Christmas stories

The Victorians enjoyed stories about Christmas. A favourite Christmas story tells of Santa Claus, short for St Nicholas. On Christmas Eve he flies through the night sky on his sledge pulled by reindeer. Children believe that he brings presents for them to open on Christmas morning.

▼ Santa talks to children in his grotto.

▶ A Victorian Christmas card shows Santa with his sledge.

▲ Scrooge (left) is visited by the Spirit of Christmas Present (right). The Spirit tells Scrooge that part of Christmas is the joy of giving.

Another story tells of Ebenezer Scrooge, a mean old man who hated Christmas. But by the end of the story Scrooge has changed into a kind person who enjoys giving to the poor at Christmas.

Christmas customs

Today, families decorate their homes with tinsel and coloured lights at Christmas. Many people have a Christmas tree in their home. Huge fir trees twinkling with lights also stand in town centres.

Special Christmas lights brighten up the streets and shops all through December. ▼

▲ These carol singers, dressed in Victorian clothes, sing in the street as people have done for hundreds of years.

Music, fun and eating delicious foods are still part of Christmas. People have parties in the weeks leading up to Christmas Day.

Christmas Eve

Christmas Eve, on December 24th, is celebrated in different ways. Children might hang a stocking at the end of their bed or over the fireplace, for Santa to fill with gifts. Often mince pies and a glass of whisky are left for him.

Many Christians celebrate Christmas Eve
at a special church service at midnight.
They sing carols to remember and
welcome the anniversary of Jesus' birth.

for Santa

CAROLS

Christmas Day

Some people exchange Christmas presents on Christmas Eve but most people like to open their gifts on Christmas morning. After opening the presents, families often eat delicious Christmas dinners.

◀ People celebrate Christmas in all sorts of places. This family has eaten Christmas dinner in an air raid shelter, which protected people from bombs during the Second World War.

▲ A modern family sits down
to enjoy Christmas dinner.

Roast turkey is usually followed
by fruit pudding. Sometimes
lucky charms are put in the
pudding. Brandy can also be
poured over it and set alight, so
the pudding seems on fire.

▲ A delicious meal – roast turkey,
vegetables and Christmas pudding,
with fruit cake, cheese and nuts.

The Christmas season

Christmas Day is followed by Boxing Day, another holiday. New Year's Eve, on December 31st, and New Year's Day, on January 1st, are also important because they celebrate new beginnings. Twelfth Night, on the eve of January 5th, is the end of Christmas.

▼ New Year celebrations. In Scotland, New Year's Eve is called Hogmanay.

▲ These homeless people are served their Christmas dinner by young voluntary workers.

Families remember those who are away from home. The father of this family is away at the First World War. ▶

Christmas is a happy time. It is especially happy for Christians who celebrate the birth of Jesus. But feelings of joy and love remind us all to think of other people. We remember that helping others is as important as opening gifts and having fun.

Glossary

Angel A messenger believed to be sent from God.

Banquet A special meal for lots of people which includes many different foods.

Festivals Days of celebration.

Lucky charms Small trinkets, such as silver coins, horseshoes and thimbles, which are supposed to bring luck.

Manger An open box or trough for horses or cattle to eat from.

Pickled To put food in vinegar to make it last longer.

Puritans Religious people in 16th and 17th centuries who had very strict rules about living.

Shepherds People who look after sheep in the fields.

Spiced To add special flavours to food.

Stable A building where horses or cattle are kept.

Symbolize To be a sign of something.

Tinsel A Christmas decoration made from a long piece of string covered with sparkly bits of foil.

Timeline

c. 800 BC –*c.* AD 600	Celtic peoples celebrate midwinter festivals in Britain and northern Europe.
c. 753 BC–*c.* AD 395	The Romans hold Saturnalia from 17th to 28th December.
c. 4 BC	Birth of Jesus.
c. AD 30	Jesus Christ put to death.
c. 58	Christian religion begins to spread.
64–311	Christians hunted down by the Romans because of their beliefs.
324	Romans converted to Christian religion. Christians begin to celebrate the birth of Jesus on 25th December.
597	Christian religion is brought to Britain.
1837	Victoria is crowned Queen of Great Britain.
c. 1841	The custom of Christmas trees is brought to Britain from Germany.
1843	Charles Dickens writes *A Christmas Carol,* which tells the story of Ebenezer Scrooge.
1914 – 1918	The First World War.
1939 – 1945	The Second World War.

Further information

Christmas by Clare Chandler (Wayland, 1996)

Christmas by T. Wood (A & C Black, 1991)

Christmas by R. Thomas (Watts, 1994)

Christmas Poetry selected by Robert Hull (Wayland, 1991)

Index